AF483084

FINALLY
I CAN USE MY VOICE!

By Monique Lewis

Illustrated by Mike Coller

To my beloved son, Quentin,

You have faced every challenge with resilience,
growing stronger and greater with each step.
Remember, with God by your side, all things
are possible. **Matthew 19:26**

In Loving memory of your grandparents,
Oswald & Emma King whose legacy of strength
and faith continues to guide and inspire us.

with heartfelt love,
Mom

In a quiet town, there lived a little boy named Noah. Noah stood out because he had a different way of communicating with the world around him. Unlike the other kids who spoke with words, Noah expressed himself through gestures, expressions, and a unique warmth that emanated from his heart. His distinctive form of communication created a special connection, setting him apart in his own wonderful way.

Noah's world was filled with love, laughter, and the support of his caring family. However, there was one thing missing - his voice. Noah couldn't say words like other children, and it made him a bit sad.

But Noah's mom, who loved him more than anything, decided she would do whatever it took to help him. At just 9 months old, doctors diagnosed him with speech delay and labeled him on the spectrum of Autism.

SYMPTOMS
TREATMENT
NOAH

The doctors also identified that Noah's journey required a unique approach, so Noah's mom started looking for ways to help him speak, approaching it from a place of detailed research. She spent countless hours researching techniques and helpful ideas to make his journey easier.

One day at Noah's daycare, a worker asked him, "What's your name?" Now, this seems like an easy question, right? But for Noah, it was a bit tricky. He tried to say his name, but it didn't come out. Noah's mom watched, feeling a mix of sadness and determination.

In that moment of struggle, something special happened. Noah may not have said his name, but he tried. And that effort sparked something magical in his journey to find his voice.

Noah's mom hugged him tight, whispering words of encouragement into his ear. She knew they had work to do, but she wasn't going to let Noah feel alone or different. She wanted to help him shine.

Noah's mom found a special way to help him talk.
They played fun games together, using gestures and
expressions to understand each other. Noah picked
it up quickly, and soon he was expressing himself
with big smiles and happy gestures.

Now, Noah's mom also discovered something interesting — certain foods and drinks could help kids like Noah talk better. So, she made a special "speech diet" for Noah. His diet was more of a vegetarian; absolutely no processed foods, fast foods, and no sugar, not even candy.

Noah's family joined in on the fun. They all sat together at the dinner table, sharing not only meals but also hopes and dreams. It became a place where they laughed, learned, and cheered for each other.

Noah and his mom also visited a speech therapist 5 days a week, who made learning to talk feel like an exciting adventure. They played games, laughed a lot, and slowly but surely, Noah's words started to bloom.

A is for Apple
Bear
FD
SQVW
PAL BHC
23

In addition to his journey towards spoken words, there was something else that brought immense joy to Noah's heart - his love for playing with dinosaurs. The small, intricately designed figures became his companions in the imaginative world he created.

His mom noticed how these prehistoric creatures sparked a gleam in Noah's eyes and encouraged his creativity.

After months of hard work and lots of cheering, Noah said his first word on October 11th, 2021. The room lit up with happiness as Noah grinned from ear to ear, proving his mom's theory right. It wasn't just a word; it was a victory, a small step that meant the world to Noah and his mom.

Aa
ankylosaurus
Bb
barionyx
Cc
carnotaurus
Dd
diplodocus
Ee
elasmosaurus
Ff
fukuisaurus
Gg
giraffatitan
Hh
hypsilophodon
Ii
ichthyosaurus
Jj
juravenator
Kk
kentrosaurus
Ll
liliensternus
Nn
Oo
oviraptor
Pp
parasaurolophus
Tt
Uu
utahraptor
Vv
velociraptor
Zz
zalmoxes
HELLO
DANGER
WILD ZONE

With his newfound voice, Noah became more confident. He talked to his friends, played games, and expressed himself in ways that amazed everyone. The town noticed Noah's journey, and all the kids began playing together.

Noah's story taught everyone an important lesson —
that being different is something to celebrate. The
town embraced each child's special journey, creating
a community filled with love and understanding.

Noah and his mom felt grateful for the love and support they received. Their journey had turned into a testimony of triumph, proving that the power of prayer and a mother's love can make anything possible.

As Noah and his mom looked back on their adventure, they realized that every challenge and every triumph had made them stronger. Noah became an inspiration to his friends, sharing his story to encourage others facing challenges. His message was simple but powerful — never give up, and always believe in the power within you.

BUS
Little King

www.ingramcontent.com/pod-product-compliance
Lightning Source LLC
Chambersburg PA
CBHW042027110726
48010CB00007B/260